ley Handb

D0227356

Pruning
Hardy Fruits

JACK WOODWARD

Cassell

The Royal Horticultural Society

THE ROYAL HORTICULTURAL SOCIETY

Cassell Educational Limited
Villiers House
41/47 Strand
London WC2N 5JE
for the Royal Horticultural Society

First published 1990

British Library Cataloguing in Publication Data
Woodward, Jack
  Pruning hardy fruits.
  1. Gardens. Fruit trees. Pruning
  I. Title
  III. Royal Horticultural Society   IV. Series
  634'.0442

  ISBN 0 304 31103 0

Photographs by Harry Baker, Institute of Horticultural Research, East Malling, Harry Smith
Collection and Michael Warren
Line drawings by Mike Shoebridge

Phototypesetting by Chapterhouse Ltd, Formby
Printed in Hong Kong by Wing King Tong Co. Ltd

Cover: apple 'Greensleeves' grown as a spindlebush
Frontispiece: peaches like 'Peregrine' are usually fan-
trained against a wall (photographs by Harry Smith
Collection)
Back cover: pear 'Williams' Bon Chretien' grown as an
espalier (photograph by Harry Baker)

Contents

The Principles of Pruning

In practice, pruning is a simple exercise involving the removal of parts of a fruit tree or bush. The key to doing the job properly is sunlight and, once that is appreciated, everything will become clear. A little elementary botany may also help in understanding the principles of pruning.

All flowering plants derive their energy for growth and reproduction from sunlight, by a process known as photosynthesis. Using light as a source of energy, chlorophyll, which gives leaves their green colour, combines carbon dioxide, extracted from the air, and water, taken from the soil, to produce sugars, starch and other more complex products. Collectively, these are known as photosynthates. For our purposes, they may be called resources or food.

The water which is extracted from the soil by the root system carries with it to the leaves many elements dissolved as salts. These elements are important in the process of photosynthesis and in the structure of the plant and fruit.

A certain amount of water is needed by the leaves to prevent them from flagging and keep them operating properly. Any excess water which remains after delivering the salts then has two routes of escape: it is released to the air by the leaves in a process known as transpiration; and it is used to transport the photosynthates or resources to other parts of the tree or bush. If there is a shortage of water, the movement of resources may stop, causing a build-up in the leaves. These are not storage organs themselves and cannot hold more than a certain level of sugars and starch. Eventually, if unrelieved, the leaves develop early autumn colouring and drop off prematurely, taking the valuable resources with them.

The movement of photosynthates proceeds on a regular basis, mostly at night. The resources go to the growing parts of the tree or bush, being used to extend the shoot and root tips, to thicken the timber and to develop the fruit buds and crop (see figure 1, p. 6). The surplus goes into reserve and is stored in the roots and branch systems of trees and bushes, for use by the leaves the following spring. This is why it is so important that roots are not damaged by

Training fruit trees against a wall maximizes the amount of light they receive

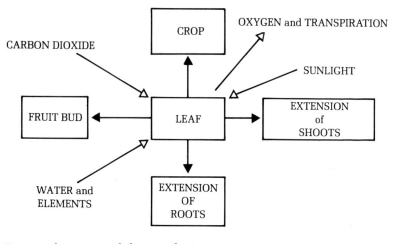

Figure 1: the process of photosynthesis

badly drained or compacted soil in winter. In a very mild winter, the roots can remain active and use up much of their reserves, leading to poor leaf formation in the spring.

In a good climate, with plenty of water and sunlight, there are enough resources to go round and satisfy all demands. With the limitations we have in Britain, however, there is competition between the various growing points, some of which are able to attract resources more easily than others. The two most powerful influences within fruit trees and bushes are shoot growth and cropping and both can inhibit the development of fruit buds and therefore the future crop. A very heavy crop takes up such a large proportion of the available resources that little is left for the development of fruit buds and growth or for putting into reserves.

The essence of pruning is to make the best use of the light we have to ensure regular cropping. This means leaving the bush or tree with sufficient reserves after cropping and leaf fall to support the next year's flowering and fruit set. All flowering and growth in early spring is dependent on reserves until the new leaves have formed and started production of photosynthates. For most soft fruits and some tree fruits which flower early and crop in mid-summer, there is enough time after the harvest for building up reserves. However, if the leaves are lost soon after harvest through pest or disease attack or lack of water, the crop the following year can be poor. Leaf spot of black currant or gooseberries can cause such a disaster. The leaves must be green, healthy and in good light and should be kept going as long as possible.

Too much shade within a tree or bush will prevent many leaves from functioning properly: they will make no contribution to the needs of the plant and may be a drain on water supplies and nutrients. Forms like the open-centre bush, cordon, espalier and spindlebush have all been developed to reduce the effect of shade.

If light is the key to pruning, water is the transporter of resources. In a very wet summer, these are moved rapidly to the growing points of the shoots, resulting in excessive growth at the expense of the roots and fruit buds. At the other extreme, a very dry summer can lead to problems, especially with shallow-rooted raspberries and trees on dwarfing rootstocks. When water is limited, the resources travel a shorter distance in a tree or bush and tend to be 'dumped' in nearby fruit or fruit buds rather than going into shoot extension. This may not matter for apples, but with raspberries the new canes for next year's crop may be too short. In a hot, dry summer, all fruit will benefit if extra water is applied over the root area and sealed in with a good mulch of organic matter.

THE PURPOSE OF PRUNING

The Oxford Dictionary says that 'to prune' is to 'trim by cutting away superfluous branches etc.'. Pruning is accepted by most gardeners as the removal of parts of the structure of a tree or bush in expectation of some beneficial result. In effect, pruning is the removal of unwanted parts, which may be shoots, branches, roots, fruit buds, damaged or diseased wood, old fruited raspberry canes or merely pieces of wood out of keeping with the form of tree being grown. Additional practices, such as tying down and fruit thinning (see p. 23), can be used as aids to pruning.

There are two main objectives in the pruning of hardy fruits:
1. To establish a young tree, bush or cane as quickly as possible in the size and shape desired, without discouraging early cropping.
2. To maintain an established tree or bush so that it can produce consistently good crops.

Fruit trees, bushes and canes would grow and produce fruit without pruning or care of any kind and they frequently have to do so in some gardens. However, the consequences of *not* pruning are that trees and bushes become tangled and overcrowded, bearing smaller, inferior fruit because of inadequate light and often doing so every other year (biennial cropping). Cane fruits – raspberries, blackberries and hybrid berries – become thickets of dead and growing canes. Pests and diseases are difficult to control and the fruit is not easy to pick, always assuming it is worth it.

The benefits of pruning are several:

1. It establishes the structure of trees and bushes in the shape required. The shortening of shoots helps to stiffen the wood and fixes the developing branches in position (see p. 17).

2. It limits the size and shape of trees and bushes to the space allocated them.

3. It removes dead, diseased or broken branches, also eliminating potential sources of infection.

4. It removes surplus or overcrowded shoots and branches to allow more light to penetrate, so improving the development of fruit buds and the colour of the fruit in apples and plums.

5. It helps to increase the size of the fruit.

6. It gives easier access, both for picking the fruit and for spraying against diseases and pests.

GROWTH CHARACTERISTICS

Fruit and vegetative buds (see figure 2, opposite)
Tree fruits carry two sorts of bud – fruit buds and vegetative buds – and it is important to be able to recognize these when pruning. The fruit buds are so called because they have the potential to produce flowers and subsequently fruit. Vegetative buds, on the other hand, normally produce only shoot growth, although occasionally, following a good summer, they can also flower. On apples and pears, there is usually a clear distinction between the two types of bud, based on size. Stone fruits – plum, cherry and peach – have buds of equal size which are more readily distinguished by shape. Fruit buds in plums also vary with variety, 'Victoria' having pointed buds.

In soft fruit, there are no such distinctions between fruit and vegetative buds. Black currants produce flowers from buds on young wood and the same buds are able to produce shoots. In the same way, red currants and gooseberries have buds on young wood capable of both fruit and growth, but they also produce spur systems (see below) which carry most of the crop.

Spur-formers and non-spur-formers
As well as being able to identify fruit buds, it is useful to know where they are formed. Hardy fruits can be roughly divided into those which fruit on one-year old wood (growth produced in the previous year) and those which crop on two-year old or older wood and are capable of forming spurs. (Autumn-fruiting raspberries are exceptional in that they fruit on the current season's growth.) Spurs are very short lengths of wood terminating in a fruit bud, sometimes

singly, but becoming much branched and complicated with age. Close examination of a spur system will reveal that it is made up of small extensions of one-year old wood, each carrying a terminal fruit bud. The division between spur-formers and non-spur-formers is not clear cut, but it separates those fruits which require good growth to perform and those which do not.

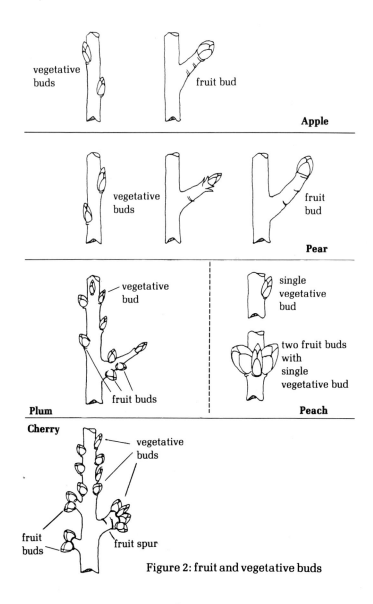

Figure 2: fruit and vegetative buds

Fruits dependent on a regular supply of new growth:

> Acid cherries
> Black currants
> Blackberries and hybrid berries
> Peaches and nectarines
> Plums and damsons (also forming
> spurs)
> Raspberries

Fruits which can form spur systems and will crop on older wood, but may require young shoots to provide replacements:

> Apples
> Gooseberries
> Pears
> Red and white currants
> Sweet cherries

Habits

The cropping and growing habits of different varieties within each type of fruit can vary considerably and, when pruning, it is necessary to take into account their natural inclinations. Trees and bushes vary from upright to spreading and drooping and clearly they need different treatments if grown without support. Grown in a formal shape such as espalier, the habit matters less.

Among apples, for example, 'Worcester Pearmain' is a stiff, fairly upright variety, producing fruit buds on the tips of young shoots (a tip-bearer), and it does not produce spurs easily, which often makes the tree look bare. By contrast, 'Golden Delicious', also a tip-bearer, spurs freely and soon develops a drooping habit from heavy cropping (see figure 6, p. 24). 'Cox's Orange Pippin' not only spurs freely but produces lots of side shoots when growing well, which gives the tree a crowded appearance.

Apical dominance

In all tree and bush fruits, the terminal or top bud of a shoot is more or less dominant over the lower buds and may in some instances prevent them from breaking into growth. This influence is known as apical dominance and it is critical to all pruning. It comes into play when pruning away the top bud or buds of an upright shoot to allow lower buds to grow out. Similarly, because the top buds of an upright shoot exert more dominance than the top buds of a flatter shoot, bending a shoot down transfers the dominance to the highest bud on the bend (see p.23).

Apical dominance is probably a result of the strength with which

Apple 'Golden Delicious' on M9 as a dwarf pyramid

plant growth substances are able to direct resources to the highest point. Notching also turns it to advantage, by creating new high points and encouraging growth where it is wanted (see p.25).

For full information about fruit-growing – including planting, feeding, propagation and control of pests and diseases; recommended varieties; and fruits not covered here, such as apricot and fig – see *The Fruit Garden Displayed* by Harry Baker (RHS/Cassell).

Pruning in Practice

PRUNING CUTS (see figure 3, below)

Young shoots and small-diameter pieces of wood can be removed by using a sharp knife or a pair of secateurs and larger branches will require a saw. The cuts, whether large or small, should be made close to a bud or side shoot without leaving a 'snag'. This is always likely to become moribund and infected with disease, which could extend down the shoot and kill the chosen bud.

Cuts into one-year old wood or current season's growth must always be made immediately above a bud or leaf. The bud selected should be on the side of the shoot where future growth is desired. When a shoot is to be removed completely, the cut needs to be made as close to its source as possible.

Large cuts are best made to a side shoot (lateral) or branch or even, as a last resort, to a fruiting spur. Occasionally, an important branch becomes devoid of side branches and it may be necessary to cut into it to stimulate growth from otherwise totally dormant buds.

All pruning cuts must be made smooth to reduce the risk of disease infection, so sharp, well maintained tools are essential. After sawing off a large branch, some trimming round the edges with a sharp knife may be required.

Figure 3: pruning cuts

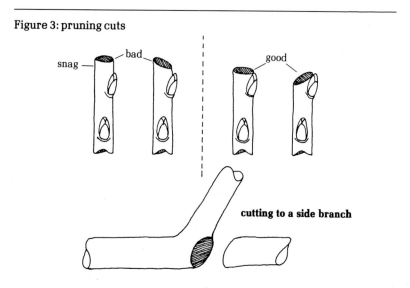

When removing a heavy branch from a tree, it is easier to carry out the task in two parts. Remove the bulk of the weight of the branch by cutting back to about 16 in. (40 cm) from its base. The final cut can then be made cleanly close to the base, avoiding the whole branch dropping uncontrollably and tearing the timber.

All pruning cuts, especially large ones, are wounds liable to infection by disease. The risk will depend on the amount of infection present near by and the natural resistance of the variety. Properly made cuts heal well, the wound covers itself naturally with protective tissue and infection is less likely. However, the application of a protective paint is an additional safeguard where silver leaf and coral spot are known to be a problem. The manufacturer's instructions should be followed carefully. (It is not the practice to protect pruning cuts on bush or cane fruits.)

PRUNING TOOLS

The tools required for pruning are sharp knives, secateurs and saws. All should be convenient for the user to handle, kept in good condition and cleaned and oiled after use. Using blunt or rusty tools can make pruning a much more difficult task than it need be.

Plum 'Reinette Claude' as a fan; stone fruits are particularly at risk from wounds

Knives

The traditional pruning knife is large and with a slightly curved blade. Some pruning knives are made with a small handle which does not always fit comfortably in the hand. Select one which has a good grip and will feel at home when in use. Although most pruning knives have a curved blade, this is not essential to successful pruning. A sharp straight blade can be just as effective and could double for grafting as well.

Knives are most useful for pruning young trees and removing undesirable shoots cleanly. To use a knife properly and safely requires some practice and dexterity, so many people will find secateurs more convenient. For removing clusters of strong shoots (water shoots) from apple trees, a sharp saw is best. Do not use a good pruning knife for cutting other materials like string, pencils and plastic, but keep it strictly for pruning work.

Secateurs

There are several types of secateurs. The most common ones rely on either a scissor action or a blade impacting on an anvil. Both are equally useful and, provided they are well maintained, should perform properly and last a long time. Before purchasing a pair of secateurs, always make sure that they can be sharpened if need be and that spares are available when required. Check that the handles and movement are comfortable to use and that any clips are out of the way of fingers when pruning.

Correctly used, a good pair of secateurs should be able to cut through wood as thick as an adult's thumb without distortion. If the cutting blade of the secateurs is kept uppermost and the free hand presses down on the wood being removed as the cut is made, less effort is required of the secateurs.

In addition to small single-handed secateurs, there are long-handled pruners or loppers for use with both hands. The cutting heads are based on the same principles as those for smaller secateurs. The handles, from 20 to 30 in. (50–75 cm) long, give good leverage and they can be used for larger cuts, for example, when making basal cuts in black currants.

Saws (see figure 4, opposite)

Grecian saw: This has a curved blade tapering to a point, which makes it useful for getting into awkward places in a tree. Older models of the Grecian saw had fine teeth set to cut as the saw was pulled and were laborious to use when not perfectly sharp, but the latest models are made of hard steel and have extremely sharp teeth (again, cutting on the return stroke). The bulk of saw work in pruning is possible with this type of saw.

Bush or bow saw: Commonly used for cutting logs in the garden, this is useful for removing large limbs beyond the scope of the Grecian saw. It must be fitted with a good-quality, sharp, clean blade.

Folding saw: There have been folding saws available for many years and they can be used instead of the Grecian saw. The blade is about 6 in. (15 cm) long and, when folded up, the saw is easily carried in the pocket. In recent years, saws have improved in design and performance and a new type of cutting edge has been introduced, which makes a very clean cut requiring no further trimming. A folding saw with the new blade is easily capable of

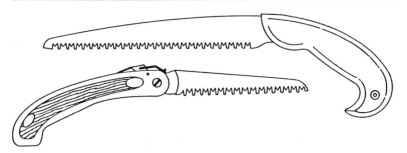

Figure 4: modern Grecian saw (*above*) and folding saw (*below*)

cutting branches up to 3 in. (8 cm) in diameter. The blade may be brittle in cold weather and will not stand too much flexing.

Long-arm pruners: These have either a secateur or saw head fixed at the end of a wooden or aluminium pole. A lever at the base of the pole operates the secateurs. The pole used can be almost any length, but is usually between 5 and 10 ft (1.5–3 m). However, pruning at a distance leads to poor-quality work. Of course, trees are always reaching for the sun, but one of the messages of pruning today is to provide easy access to the fruit. A fruit tree which needs a long-arm pruner should be viewed critically.

Additional aids

These include string, for tying in shoots or branches (a fat soft string, such as fillis or baler twine, avoids abrasion to the bark); weighted or unweighted clothes pegs to help bend shoots of closely planted trees (see p. 25); and a walking stick or similar to pull down shoots for inspection or pruning.

Times of Pruning

All pruning has a dwarfing effect. A tree or bush which has been pruned regularly will be smaller than an unpruned one, given the same conditions and level of cropping. The severity of this dwarfing effect depends on the time of year when the tree or bush is pruned and on the amount of wood or leaf removed. There are three main times for pruning – in the winter, in the spring after bud burst (i.e. just as the buds break into growth) and during the summer from mid-July onwards. Summer and spring pruning both have a greater dwarfing effect than winter pruning.

WINTER PRUNING

Newly planted trees and bushes
Newly planted apples, pears, currants, gooseberries and raspberries can all be pruned during the first winter. (For details, see individual chapters.)

The first pruning is the time to select shoots for branch formation (except with an unfeathered maiden, where this has to be delayed a year; see p. 33). On open-centre bush red currants, gooseberries, apples and pears, the shoots chosen for branch formation are traditionally cut by a third or a quarter. This causes a number of buds to grow out into side shoots (laterals), helping to stiffen the future branch (see figure 5, p. 18). Laterals may then be used as secondary branches or induced to form spurs. Any shoots selected for permanent branch formation on apples and pears should be at right angles to the centre stem of the tree, to ensure a strong link; narrow-angled branches are much weaker and liable to break under the weight of the first decent crop. Of course, espaliers and fans do not have such limitations.

It is a mistake to believe that hard pruning of newly planted or young trees and bushes will speed up growth and cropping. Pruning not only reduces the size of a tree or bush but delays and lessens cropping, and winter pruning is no exception, even though the overall appearance is one of growth. Therefore, if the object is to

A four-tier espalier pear (*above*) and three-tier espalier apple (*below*); summer pruning is important to control growth

cover space quickly and pick fruit as soon as possible, the lighter the pruning the better.

Established trees and bushes
Winter is the time to restore order. In the absence of leaves, it is easier to see broken and diseased pieces of wood and branches which have become awkward or out of place. For example, the very low wood on some black currant varieties, which tend to prostrate themselves with cropping, can be removed and very often that is all

Figure 5: the effects of pruning

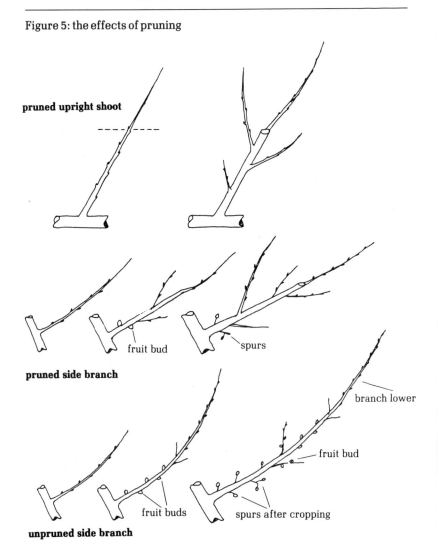

pruned upright shoot

fruit bud

spurs

pruned side branch

branch lower

fruit bud

unpruned side branch

fruit buds

spurs after cropping

the pruning required. The open-centre gooseberry bush can be 'opened', by cutting back internal shoots to spurs so that it is easier to pick. On tree fruits, pieces of timber which make harvesting difficult or will be difficult to harvest from can be removed.

The importance of light has already been mentioned. Winter is also the time to ensure that the branches, laterals and shoots are so distributed and selected that light will be able to reach all parts when the whole is covered with leaves. The centre of a tree must not be allowed to fill up with vertical shoots arising from the top sides of branches, for these create shade, compete for resources and are less productive than flatter shoots. A centre-leader tree like a spindlebush will have to be pruned to keep it open and prevent the top shading the lower parts. Crossing wood is best removed or reduced. When pruning trees, arrange the branches and laterals so that they radiate from the centre like spokes of a wheel.

Winter pruning can also be used to increase the size of fruit on apples and pears. This is done by simply reducing the number of fruit buds on the tree, which raises the leaves-to-fruit ratio the following summer. More leaves mean more resources to each apple or pear. Thus, in formal arrangements such as espaliers and cordons, the summer-pruned laterals or spurs are cut back to one or two fruit buds. On open-centre bush or spindlebush apples or pears, the two-year old or older laterals can be cut back to a fruit bud to form a long spur. The length of the long spur is a matter of judgement as to the number of fruit buds to be left on the tree.

In the case of apples, a balanced winter pruning improves not only the size of the fruit but also its colour, by allowing better light. Under no circumstances, however, should the quantity of fruit buds on a tree be reduced to scarcity level. If in doubt, it is better to be sure of a crop and larger fruit by fruit thinning in June (see p. 23).

SPRING PRUNING

After bud burst and during flowering is the time to prune stone fruits – plums, cherry and peach – as there is then less risk of infection from silver leaf disease and the wounds heal more quickly. Newly planted or young trees are best pruned close to bud burst, when the cutting has less of a retarding effect on growth than it would later on during flowering. Older trees are normally pruned at flowering time.

When pruning stone fruits to create a framework of branches, it is most important to select wide-angled shoots for the purpose. Apart from the danger of narrow-angled branches breaking under the weight of the crop later on, there is the further hazard of bacterial canker, especially in susceptible cherry varieties.

Unlike winter pruning, which prompts buds to break into growth as the apical dominance is removed, pruning after bud burst delays the growth of buds. As the season advances towards flowering, the greater is the delay in growth. This can be turned to advantage with mature apple and pear trees that have reached their limits. It has now become common practice to leave the tops unpruned in winter and to remove them after bud burst, which puts a stop to the higher growth for a time and admits more light into the lower parts.

SUMMER PRUNING

Pruning in the summer months removes part of the current season's growth, with leaves attached, taking away some of the productive capacity of the tree or bush. For this reason, it is an effective method of controlling growth and has a strong dwarfing effect. Summer pruning can also improve the colour of fruit on certain apple varieties by admitting more light, but it can reduce the crop and the size of the fruit if overdone.

Summer pruning has been used for many years for the formation and control of formal arrangements like espaliers, cordons and dwarf pyramids. It has also been introduced as an aid to control growth in freer-growing systems, such as the spindlebush.

The Modified Lorette System, applied to restricted forms of apples and pears, requires the cutting of mature lateral shoots arising directly from the branches to three leaves above the basal cluster of leaves. The shoots cut must be woody at the base and exceeding 8 in. (20 cm) in length. Since shoots vary in growth and maturity, this may mean going over the tree several times during the summer. Any shoots arising from spurs or side shoots are cut to one leaf above the basal cluster. This keeps the tree compact within its allocated space and ensures that good light reaches all parts.

On dwarf pyramid plums, summer pruning of the shoots selected for forming branches strengthens the wood and makes it less likely to break under the weight of the crop. Traditional plum tree forms like the open-centre bush may also be summer pruned with the same advantages.

Many gardens will have large vigorous trees of no specific shape, some inherited from previous owners, others the result of planting on a too vigorous rootstock. The problem with such a tree is that its vigour makes it unproductive. It can be greatly improved by summer pruning, which entails the removal of one-, two- and three-year old vertical shoots, especially in the top of the tree, leaving flatter shoots and branches unpruned. This will redistribute resources where they are needed and allow more light into the lower parts of the tree; it should improve the colour of the fruit, in apples, the formation of fruit buds and future cropping. However, a tree carrying a heavy crop should never be summer pruned, as this would result in smaller fruit and fewer fruit buds.

With apples, a side benefit of summer pruning is to reduce the risk of bitter pit. This disorder is caused by calcium deficiency in the fruit and shows up as brown sunken spots on the surface and brown areas in the flesh. Removing the growing tips of shoots lowers the demand for calcium so that more is available for the fruit.

As a rule, summer pruning starts in mid-July for pears and a week later for apples in the south of England and in August further north. With plums, it is usually carried out in late July. The later the start the less risk there is of regrowth.

A dwarf pyramid plum

21

Special Techniques

FRUIT THINNING

Fruit thinning is a most effective way of getting trees – apples, pears, plums and peaches – to crop regularly and is an important accompaniment to pruning. By preventing overloading of the tree, it encourages growth and the formation of fruit buds, as well as increasing the size of the fruit and improving its colour for the current harvest. Young trees in particular need to have fruit numbers limited, or they will take longer to become established.

To get the best results from thinning, the operation should be carried out as soon as possible after the fruit has set. With apples and pears, there is usually a drop of small fruitlets and unset flowers after flowering has finished and the remaining fruitlets then begin to make rapid growth. As a rough guide, apples, pear and plum fruitlets will be just under ½ in. (12 mm) in diameter when it is time to thin. Thinning each cluster to a single fruitlet may be sufficient in some years, because a further natural drop may take place. However, apples benefit from being reduced to one every alternate cluster, since they require more leaves per fruit.

TYING DOWN (see figure 6, p. 24)

Tying down or bending shoots and branches is another application of the principle of apical dominance and is based on the fact that horizontal growth is likely to be more fruitful, while vertical growth tends to be more vigorous and unproductive. A tree with its branches flattened to below 40° above the horizontal also has a much greater spread and therefore a better opportunity to carry a good crop. Tying down is a useful way of getting young trees of apples, pears and plums to fruit and so reduce vigour and can be used in the same way on old over-vigorous trees. The cropping reduces the vigour, not the tying down.

For trees which are to have a definite structure, such as an open-centre bush or a four-branch spindlebush (see p. 38), the selected branches can be lowered into position in the second year after

---

Apples, 'Sturmer Pippin' open-centre bush (*above*) and 'Golden Delicious', spindle bush (*below*)

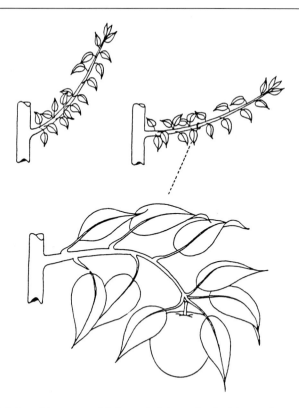

Figure 6: (*above*) two-year old shoot tied down for fruiting and spread; (*below*) tip-bearing apple, with the shoot bent by the weight of the fruit

planting. If the branches have not been pruned, they may remain supple enough for a further year's growth before tying down. The string must be secured so that the branch is kept straight without bending. This means attaching the string at about the middle of the branch, where it has some strength. Lowering branches becomes more difficult as they become more woody and, for this reason, they should be checked in August for signs of stiffening. Most apple varieties, like 'Cox's Orange Pippin' and 'Bramley's Seedling', are best with the branches first set at 40° above the horizontal. This allows for further fall under the increasing weight of the branch and the crop. However, tip-bearing varieties which tend to droop, such as 'Golden Delicious' and 'Jonagold', may need tying up rather than down once the trees fruit. Careful selection of branches is still important and narrow-angled branches cannot be improved by tying down (see also figure 10, p. 30).

The actual tying down is done by tying a piece of string round the base of the support stake and then attaching the other end to the lowered branch, using a non-slip loop or bowline and placing it outside a lateral or small spur to prevent it from slipping down the branch. In time, the weight of the branch slackens the string and it can be removed. If there are a number of branches to be secured, attachment to the stake can be simplified by driving a small nail or staple into the base of the post and tying all the strings at once. Under no circumstances should string be tied round the trunk of the tree in case it causes abrasions or constriction. If a stake is not used for support, a tent peg or skewer driven well into the soil is satisfactory, except in very wet and windy conditions.

Tying down can also be used for closely planted spindlebush trees on very dwarfing M9 or M27 rootstocks, to contain them within their allotted space.

A substitute for tying down on young shoots is to use small weights. For soft growing shoots in the summer, the weight of a clothes peg at the end of the shoot is sufficient, but stronger wood may need additional weight attached to the peg. On more substantial branches, much heavier weights can be used. The advantage of clothes pegs is that they can be quickly attached and then moved on as soon as the shoot has been fixed in position.

NOTCHING (see figure 7, below)

Notching is an old practice still used occasionally to induce a dormant bud to grow out. A small piece of bark and wood is removed about ½ in. (12 mm) above the bud, using a sharp knife. If the cut is made too close to the bud, the shoot produced grows out at a narrower angle. The cut must not be too deep but should just penetrate the wood below the outer bark. A V-shaped cut gives a clear view of the depth of cut. Notching is most useful in the formation of trees where the emergence of a shoot is essential, as when creating espaliers, or when growing varieties which are reluctant to produce laterals. It is usually carried out in late winter.

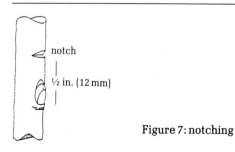

notch

½ in. (12 mm)

Figure 7: notching

STUBBING (see figure 8, below)

Often when pruning a tree, a well sited branch or shoot has to be removed because it has grown badly or is damaged and, in the case of the spindlebush, branches have to be removed periodically to create space and for replacement purposes. To remove shoots and branches completely in the winter with a pair of secateurs is not easy nor is it always desirable: usually a small stub is left, which will produce regrowth that tends to go straight up. Therefore, if a replacement shoot is required to grow out horizontally, it is best to make a flat horizontal cut like the lip of a jug. This is known as stubbing and is carried out when winter pruning.

Figure 8: stubbing

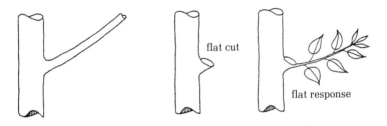

flat cut

flat response

DEHORNING

When trees have become too tall or too wide, branches can be cut back to laterals growing in the desired direction. This is known as dehorning and is usually carried out in winter. Used in conjunction with summer pruning, it can improve the access of light to a tree and make it more accessible for spraying and picking. Whenever a branch is cut back, there is always a vigorous local response of mainly upright shoots with a number of flatter shoots. Summer pruning removes the most vigorous and the weaker flatter ones can be left to develop fruit buds and perhaps be tied down into better positions. It is not advisable to dehorn all the limbs on a tree in one year and the treatment should be spread over two years at least.

BARK-RINGING (see figure 9, opposite)

Bark-ringing consists of removing a section of bark from the trunk or main branch of a tree to interrupt the passage of photosynthates to the root system and compel their use in the formation of fruit buds. It is used on over-vigorous apples and pears but not on stone fruits because of the risk of disease.

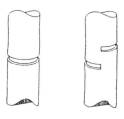

Figure 9: bark-ringing – (*left*) a complete ring, (*right*) two half-rings

The operation is best carried out in May or during flowering, when the sap is flowing and the bark is easily removed. A ring of bark is cut out with a sharp knife, making the cut so that it just reaches the wood to free the strip of bark. The width of the cut will depend on the size of the tree, ranging from slightly over ½ in. (12 mm) for a large tree to ¼ in. (6 mm) for a small tree. After removing the ring, cover the cut with plastic adhesive tape. The wound will heal over by midsummer, when the tape can be removed. It is very important that the wound should heal properly. A less risky but equally effective method is to leave about 1 in. (2.5 cm) of bark intact so that the ring is incomplete or to make two half-rings at different points.

Bark-ringing is used as a last resort to induce bearing in a particularly unfruitful vigorous tree, when other methods such as summer pruning have failed. All the conditions – adequate pollination, correct nutrition and kind climate – must be right for good fruit set or the beneficial effects of the ringing will soon be lost.

An espalier can be started with the help of notching to encourage strategic shoots

ROOT-PRUNING

Root-pruning is a desperate measure taken with over-vigorous unfruitful trees, including plums, when the strength of the root system is too great for the top and for the space allocated. The reasons may be that the tree has been grafted on a vigorous rootstock, which will grow luxuriantly in good soil, or that the scion (the part of the tree which is the fruiting variety) has bypassed the rootstock and produced its own roots. In most cases of excessive vigour, failure to crop is the basic cause and the fact that resources are going into growth not fruit. Such trees are usually best dug up and replaced with a better combination of rootstock and scion.

Root-pruning is carried out in the dormant period when there are no leaves on the trees. Only the major roots – the thick woody ones – are cut, leaving the thin fibrous roots undamaged. The roots are located by digging a circular trench approximately 3¼ ft (1 m) from the trunk. Then cut every alternate major root, removing a section of it completely with a saw or a pair of heavy-duty secateurs. The uncut roots are marked with a small cane before refilling the trench and, if the tree continues to grow strongly, these can be uncovered and cut the following winter. This method of root-pruning in stages prevents the tree from becoming too unstable.

Double-U cordon apples

Apples

Apple trees available to the amateur gardener are grafted or budded onto four different rootstocks – MM106, M26, M9 and M27, in descending order of vigour. In most modern gardens, apples on MM106 will make a tree too big for comfort and the very dwarfing M9 or even extremely dwarfing M27 will be more suitable. However, in light or poor soil, where trees on M9 do not do well, the more vigorous MM106 may be essential. Unfortunately, this will only emerge with experience and at some cost. Some nurserymen sell trees on MM106 because they do survive in gardens and fewer complaints are received; when the tree is fully grown, it is too late to complain. Always purchase trees from a reputable nursery or garden centre which sells certified trees with known rootstocks.

The choice of rootstock is important because it influences not only the size and manageability of the tree, but also its fruit-bearing. In general, the more dwarfing the rootstock the sooner the young tree will bear fruit.

Another consideration is the type of tree to be bought. Trees are sold as either one-year old 'maidens' or two- or three-year old partially trained trees. One-year old trees are 'feathered' or 'un-feathered', that is to say they have or do not have side shoots (see figures 10, 11 and 12, pp. 30, 34 and 35). The number of feathers on a maiden depends on rootstock and variety, with vigorous rootstocks producing most feathers. Where possible, it is wise to buy a well feathered tree, which allows shoots to be selected for branch formation at the time of planting and thereby saves a year.

Feathering characteristics

MANY FEATHERS	INTERMEDIATE	FEW FEATHERS
Cox's Orange Pippin	Ashmead's Kernel	Bramley's Seedling
Gala	Discovery	Epicure
Golden Delicious	Egremont Russet	Grenadier
Greensleeves	Jonagold	Saint Edmund's Pippin
James Grieve	Katy	Spartan
Kent	Lane's Prince Albert	Warner's King
Sunset	Ribston Pippin	Worcester Pearmain
Suntan	Sturmer Pippin	

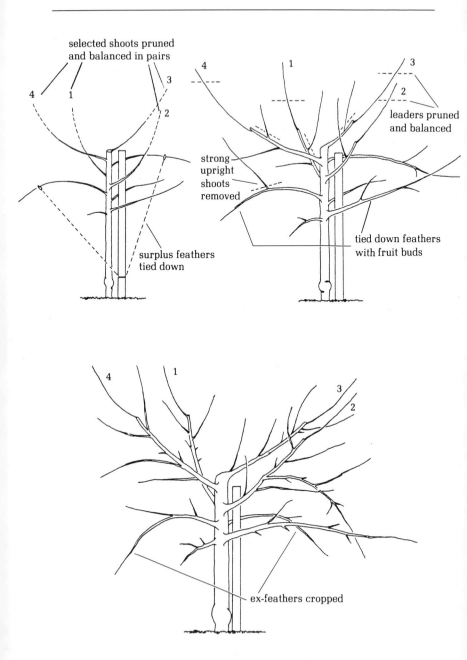

Figure 10: four-branch open-centre apple tree from a feathered maiden –
(*above left*) at planting; (*above right and below*) first and second winter
after planting

Finally, a decision must be made on the form of tree to be grown, for this will affect its pruning and training. There are two main groups – unrestricted forms, which are grown in the open; and restricted forms, which are grown against walls or fences or on wires. Open-centre bush, half-standard, standard and spindlebush belong to the first category; cordon, espalier and dwarf pyramid belong to the second and are particularly suitable where space is limited.

OPEN-CENTRE BUSH, HALF-STANDARD AND STANDARD

There are few differences between the formation of an open-centre bush, half-standard and standard tree once the length of stem has been decided. Today, the commonly grown open-centre bush has a 'leg' (the distance between ground level and the first branches) of about 30 in. (75 cm). Accepted legs for half-standard and standard trees are 4½ ft (1.4 m) and 6 ft (1.8 m) respectively, but both grow too large for most situations. However, many old open-centre or vase-shaped trees still to be seen in private gardens have a leg as short as 12 in. (30 cm). (See also p. 22.)

To prune a feathered maiden (see figure 10, opposite)
After planting, in the winter, select three or four feathers at the appropriate height to start the main branches of the tree, ensuring that they have good wide angles to the central stem. It is a good idea to look down on the tree from above and mark a pair of feathers roughly opposite each other and a further pair at right angles to those. The feathers are better spaced a little apart on the central stem, rather than close to each other. If it is not possible to find four feathers, three will do so long as they are equally spaced.

Cut off the main stem immediately above the top chosen feather and then prune this and the other two or three selected feathers, always cutting to an outward-facing bud. About one third is the optimum amount to remove, but it helps to balance the tree if the height of the cuts above ground level is the same for each feather or at least for each pair of feathers. This may mean cutting about a half away in some instances and only a quarter in others. The surplus feathers can be removed cleanly with a sharp knife. However, in the interests of getting the tree established and early cropping, they are better left unpruned and should be tied down before growth starts, out of the way of the selected branches.

In the first year, every encouragement must be given to the tree to make growth, by applying a good mulch and watering if necessary. During August, check that the feathers, or leading shoots as they have become, are going in the direction required: the future branches should develop at an angle not more than 40° above the horizontal. Tying down with string will help to correct any deviations, but may not be necessary until the second year in the ground.

The first winter after planting, the leading shoot at the end of each developing branch must be cut back to an outward-facing bud, removing a quarter to a third. This helps to fix the branch in position. A balance must still be maintained between the pairs of branch leaders when pruning them to prevent one from becoming dominant. The second shoot on the branch is removed completely, but any other shoots are left unpruned unless they are strongly upright. Once the tied-down feathers have cropped, they are removed, usually in the second winter after planting.

The pruning of the leading shoots continues until the tree has filled its allocated space, when they are left to develop fruit buds along their full length. To prevent continued expansion of the tree after this, it is worth either tying down the leading shoots or summer pruning them to five leaves from the point of origin.

As the main branches extend, the distance between them increases and this space is filled with secondary branches and fruiting laterals. These must not prevent access into the tree and should be encouraged to grow radially outwards, either by selecting suitable branches when pruning or by tying in. Some of the more upright varieties can be assisted to crop by tying down the laterals in a flatter position. In practice, laterals should not be more than four years of age to produce the best-quality fruit, but much will depend on how easily spurs are formed or whether they have to be encouraged. The treatment of laterals can be 'rule of thumb'. In general, however, all strong-growing vertical shoots are removed in July, while other shoots are left for two years and then cut back to the two-year old wood or to a fruit bud in winter; the length of shoot retained is immaterial as long as it has space. This starts to form a spur system. Special care should be taken to preserve the flatter shoots, but if there is a shortage of breaks (i.e. of buds producing shoots), some of the more upright shoots must be kept and tied down. In the early development of a tree in years when the crop is light, there is always a tendency to produce strong upright growth. This growth must be controlled by summer pruning and preferably removed completely. The density of the shoots in full leaf should be such that on a bright midsummer day the ground beneath the tree is covered with dappled shade.

Trees which feather freely as maidens usually spur freely (see p. 29). Pruning to induce spurs is done by either cutting laterals of the current season's growth to five leaves in late July or August, or cutting two-year old laterals to five fruit buds in winter. Once established, the spurs are winter pruned to two buds and any subsequent shoots are summer pruned to five leaves. Periodically, the spur systems will have to be rejuvenated, by removing some of the fruit buds and cutting the structure closer to the main branch.

To prune a poorly feathered maiden
Often trees on the M9 rootstock do not have enough good feathers to choose from to form branches. The easiest solution is to put off making a decision. Cut the tree to a bud 4 in. (10 cm) above the top feather and then stub all narrow-angled feathers. Treat the tree well in the summer, feeding it and watering in dry conditions, to encourage good breaks. It should then be possible to select four feathers as leading shoots in the winter and proceed as above.

To prune an unfeathered maiden (see figure 11, p. 34)
Unfeathered maidens are frequently difficult to start because a cut may not produce the breaks required. Recent developments in nurseries have improved the feathering of some varieties like 'Bramley's Seedling', but it is still common to get unfeathered trees. Although a good, strong, tall, unfeathered tree can be induced to make the right breaks, a weak tree is not so amenable.

After planting, locate the position on the tree from which it is intended to start the branches. Select four buds positioned at right angles to one another on the central stem, marking each with a small piece of adhesive tape. Remove the two buds immediately above the top chosen bud and then cut off the main stem above the next bud. Cut a notch ½ in. (12 mm) above each of the four selected buds. The shoots produced should grow out at good angles to form the main branches. The following winter, the extension above the top shoot is removed cleanly. It is always necessary to give the tree every encouragement to grow during the first summer and inducing vigour by extra feeding is one way of pushing the buds into growth.

Treatment of two-year old trees
Nurserymen and garden centres often have two-year old and older trees available. These are either specially grown for the garden centre trade or are nursery trees which have been left unsold as maidens and pruned back in situ to grow a further year. There is nothing wrong with such trees and, in the case of poorly feathering varieties, it is a good way to start. The important thing is to make sure that the tree has produced shoots which can be used to form the framework of the future tree.

After planting, treat as for a feathered maiden, removing narrow-angled branches, choosing the shoots for branch formation and tying down the surplus. Pruning of the selected shoots must be light and removal of a quarter of the length is quite adequate.

With half-standard and standard trees, the framework is usually already formed at the time of purchase and it is a matter of selecting and encouraging what is present to grow in the direction required. If a maiden tree is bought with the intention of growing it on a longer leg, allow the central leader to grow to the necessary height, probably over two seasons, and support it with a cane.

Figure 11: four-branch open-centre apple tree from an unfeathered maiden – (*above*) at planting; (*below*) first and second winter after planting

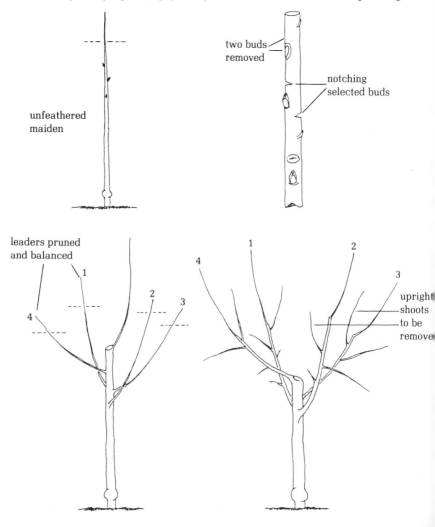

DWARF PYRAMID (see figure 12, below, and p. 11)

The dwarf pyramid has a central leader from which, at about 1 ft (30 cm) from the ground, the branches radiate, tapering to the top in a pyramid shape. Trees on the more dwarfing rootstocks will require good support with stakes or horizontal wires on posts.

Planting a well feathered tree gives a good start to the formation of a dwarf pyramid. After planting, the main stem of the tree is cut to a bud 4 in. (10 cm) above the top feather and all narrow-angled feathers are stubbed back. Feathers over 1 ft (30 cm) long are cut by half to an outward-facing bud and the rest left unpruned.

In the second winter, the leading shoot should be cut to 1 ft (30 cm) to promote further laterals to break. It is the usual practice to cut it to a bud on the opposite side to the previous year's cut, in order to keep the central leader straight, although this is not absolutely necessary if the tree is well supported. Any narrow-angled branches must be removed or stubbed, as well as low branches. The central leader is shortened thus each winter, leaving 1 ft (30 cm) of new growth, until it has reached the desired height; it is then pruned in May or during the summer to restrict growth.

Figure 12: dwarf pyramid apple from a poorly feathered maiden – (*left*) at planting; (*centre and right*) first and second winter after planting

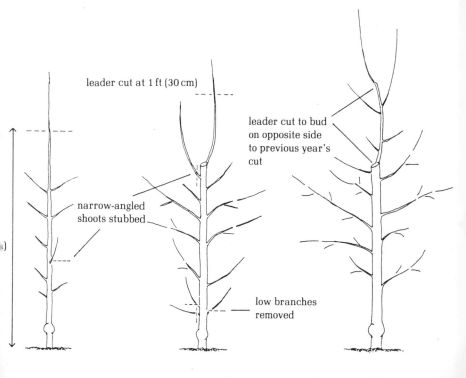

leader cut at 1 ft (30 cm)

leader cut to bud on opposite side to previous year's cut

narrow-angled shoots stubbed

low branches removed

To contain a dwarf pyramid tree and form a close spur system, summer pruning is essential from the second season onwards. In late July or early August, the branch leaders are cut to five leaves and lateral shoots over 8 in. (20 cm) long are cut to three leaves above the basal cluster of leaves. Any shoots arising from spurs are cut to one leaf. The spur system on a mature dwarf pyramid may need reducing to two or three buds per spur in the winter, to maintain the quality of the fruit and the vigour of the tree.

When an unfeathered or poorly feathered maiden is used, cut the tree at planting to 2 ft (60 cm) or 31 in. (80 cm) to start the branches low down. The second bud from the top can be removed with advantage. Pruning then follows the same pattern as for a feathered tree, except that special measures may be necessary if insufficient laterals are produced, such as notching some buds.

CORDON (see figure 13, below)

The cordon is a versatile method of growing fruit in the garden and takes several different forms. It may be single- or multiple-stemmed and trained vertically, horizontally, obliquely or in a U-shape. The oblique cordon achieves the best balance between growth and fruit bud production. (See also p. 28 and p. 64).

The tree may be bought as a feathered or unfeathered maiden or a two- or three-year old tree and is planted pointing in the direction required. For oblique cordons, the angle to the ground should be 40–45°. On older trees and well feathered maidens, the laterals are cut to three buds on planting, leaving the leader uncut. Unfeathered or poorly feathered trees may require pruning of the leader to produce laterals, shortening it by up to one third, or some notching.

Once established, the objective of pruning a cordon is to develop a close spur system. This is achieved by limiting the spurs by winter

Figure 13: oblique cordon apple from a poorly feathered maiden –
(*left*) at planting;
(*right*) first winter after planting

leader not
usually cut

cut to three
buds

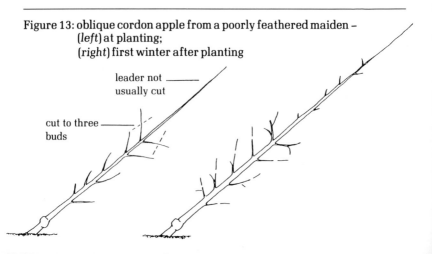

The most useful cordon is a single-stem trained obliquely

pruning and by summer pruning the laterals, shortening those over 8 in. (20 cm) long to three leaves above the basal cluster and the shoots from spurs to one leaf. The timing of summer pruning is critical and the later it can be left the better, to avoid unwanted regrowth. Any very strong verticals should be removed completely.

ESPALIER (see figure 14, pp. 38–9, and p. 16)

The tree which is known as an 'espalier' today has a central leader and a series of parallel horizontal branches trained against a wall or post-and-wire structure, although strictly speaking the supporting wires or rails themselves form the espalier. Espalier trees can be bought partially trained, with the first two or three tiers started, but they are not difficult to grow from a maiden tree.

After planting an unfeathered maiden, select a pair of outward-facing buds to produce the lowest tier of branches and cut off the main stem to a bud 4 in. (10 cm) above them. The buds are then encouraged to grow by notching ½ in. (12 mm) above each one. Growth from any buds other than the chosen pair and the top one is pinched back to three leaves and totally removed the following winter. Each winter, the process is repeated, selecting another pair of buds on the central leader 14–18 in. (35–45 cm) above the previous year's pair until the final tier is reached. On completion, new growth on the central leader is removed in May.

The developing branches are encouraged to grow by tying them at an angle of 45° to the main stem and are only lowered to the final horizontal position when they have reached the required length. The leaders on the side branches must not be pruned or the timber becomes too rigid to be lowered easily. Once the first tier has been formed, the laterals are summer pruned as for a cordon to create a close spur system (see p. 37). It is particularly important with an espalier to control vigorous growth from the top tier of branches: any strong vertical shoots must be removed completely in the summer, unless they can be tied down to fill a gap.

A feathered maiden gives some opportunity for the first tier or two to be selected from the feathers at planting. If there is no bud on the central stem to leave for the future leader, a feather can be tied in as the leader and a bud chosen on it. Then continue as above.

SPINDLEBUSH (see figure 15, pp. 40–41, and p. 22)

The spindlebush is a cone-shaped centre-leader tree developed by German and Dutch fruit growers. In its simplest form, it is made up

Figure 14: espalier apple from a well feathered maiden – (*left*) at planting; (*right*) first winter after planting; (*opposite left*) developing branches tied at 45°; (*opposite right*) two completed tiers lowered into place

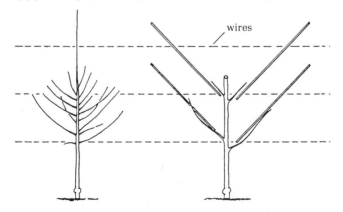

An espalier can be modified to form a palmette, with the branches tied as for an oblique cordon

of three permanent branches and a central stem (or branch) supported by a stake, but the number of branches need not be fixed.

After planting, the maiden tree is cut back to a bud at 31–35 in. (80–90 cm), to encourage buds to break and the three or four feathers selected for branch formation to grow. In a well feathered tree, it is usual to cut 4 in. (10 cm) above the top feather. However, if this is too far above the feathers to be used for branches, it may be necessary to cut further back to the feather above the chosen feathers and to tie this in as the leader and prune it. Selected feathers which are more than 16 in. (40 cm) long should be pruned back by not more than a quarter. The surplus feathers are either removed if they are narrow-angled or bent down and tied out of the way to bud up and crop before being pruned out.

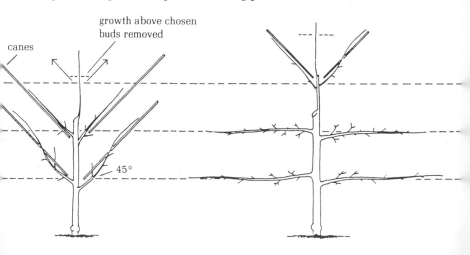

In the second winter, the central leader is pruned by one third to one quarter, depending on how the tree has grown and the number of laterals produced. The more the central leader is suppressed, the more shoots will be stimulated lower down. Any strong upright competitors to the central leader are removed or stubbed, as are any vertical shoots arising elsewhere.

In August of the second year, the framework branches are tied down to less than 40° above the horizontal so that they are roughly balanced. No summer pruning is necessary at this stage. Pruning of the central leader continues each winter until it gets beyond reach – say 6½ ft (2 m), when it is left unpruned and allowed to produce fruit buds and crop, being periodically replaced by another shoot from lower down. Meanwhile, the lower permanent branches are encouraged to spread and fill the space allocated and some of the fruiting laterals and spurs between them will be stubbed back from time to time to prevent overcrowding. Drooping timber which has cropped and 'run out of steam' must be cut hard back or removed in winter. If the lower framework is too thinly covered with fruiting laterals, some more upright shoots should be tied down into the spaces. In principle, no strong vertical shoots are allowed.

The central leader produces laterals with good angles as it grows and these are retained to form fruiting units. Narrow-angled shoots are best removed, but may be bent down for cropping if there is room. No branches on the central stem above the main framework of branches are to be considered permanent and, as soon as they reach ¾ in. (20 mm) or the thickness of a man's thumb, they should be removed by stubbing.

The main practical problem with the spindlebush, as with many centre-leader trees, is the vigour which it can produce from the tree head, especially if it is grown on the MM106 rootstock. It is

Figure 15: three- to four-branch spindlebush apple – (*left and centre*) at planting; (*right and opposite*) first, second and third winter after planting

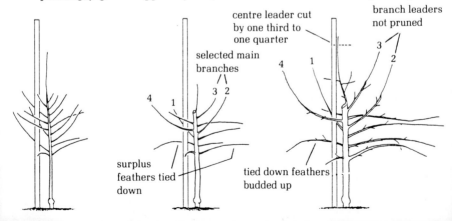

An example of a spindlebush apple

important to prevent this happening by removing all over-vigorous one-, two- or three-year old growths in late July or August and to maintain good light into the bottom of the tree. The central leader of a spindlebush is used like a pump – reduce its height and the lower branches grow, allow it to grow taller and the lower branches decline. A heavy crop slows everything down.

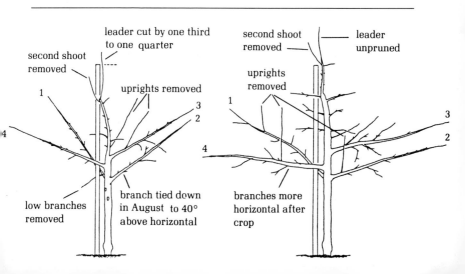

Pears

Pears are traditionally grown on Quince A or Quince C rootstocks. Quince A is normally considered the more vigorous of the two, but there is little to choose between them now with virus-free material and both produce pear trees with less vigour than MM106 for apples. Some gardens possess old pear trees of great size, which could be on seedling pear rootstocks. Pear trees are not grafted on seedling rootstocks today for obvious reasons.

All the tree forms described for apples, including spindlebush, can be used for pears with little modification, although they generally have a more upright habit and benefit from tying down shoots and branches. Maiden pear trees, especially 'Conference', do not feather as freely as some apples and, for this reason, it is often wise to seek two-year old trees for planting.

Most pears produce spur systems freely and will withstand harder cutting than apples, so they are quite amenable when confined to restricted forms. These will need and benefit from summer pruning at times. For tree forms like the open-centre bush and the larger centre-leader trees, a simple procedure of long-spur pruning is satisfactory.

LONG-SPUR PRUNING

All conveniently placed laterals are allowed to develop for two years, which permits the formation of fruit buds on the two-year old wood. In winter, the two-year old laterals are cut back to a fruit bud, usually leaving a spur of about 8 in. (20 cm). By varying the length of the spurs, the amount of fruit buds in a tree can be controlled and this is one of the advantages of long-spurring pears. Once a spur has had a good crop, it can be started again by cutting hard back.

RESTRICTED FORMS

Espalier and cordon pears will need summer pruning to control growth. Pears respond favourably to summer pruning by the Modified Lorette System. Pruning can start in the second half of July, shortening the leaders to five leaves and all strong laterals as they mature to three leaves above the basal cluster of leaves. The laterals will probably have to be more than 10 in. (25 cm) long to

Dwarf pyramid pears in bloom

have hardened at their base. Short laterals arising from the spurs which have ceased growing may be left unpruned, unless they are crowded and need thinning out, which is done by cutting a proportion of them to one leaf above the basal cluster.

In winter, the spurs are pruned to leave a good spread of fruit buds throughout the tree and much of the remnants of summer pruning will be removed. (See also p. 16.)

Plums, Gages, Damsons and Bullaces

Plums are the most commonly grown of the group of stone fruits, which includes gages (or dessert plums) and the smaller-fruited damsons and bullaces. All can be treated in the same way. Most of the plums being planted or already planted in gardens are on St Julien A rootstock. This makes a fairly vigorous tree, which can be grown and trained as an open-centre bush, half-standard, standard or large centre-leader tree, as for apples. In addition, plums may be grown as dwarf pyramid, fan and palmette. The essential difference between plums and apples is that, whereas apples may be pruned at any time, plums must not be pruned in the dormant season because of the risk of silver leaf disease. Except for summer pruning, they are usually pruned in early spring when flowering or in May. Most pruning is done in the first years to form a framework. Once an open-centre bush on St Julien A is established, it will not require more than a tidy up immediately after harvest to remove broken branches and a light thinning out each May.

When growing plums, it is worth bearing in mind the habit of growth, which is more varied than that of apples or pears. 'Victoria' tends to droop as the tree begins to crop, whereas many of

Three-year old plum 'Victoria' on Pixy as a dwarf pyramid

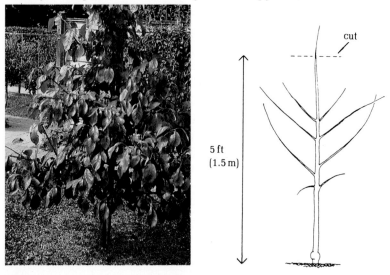

cut

5 ft
(1.5 m)

the gages remain fairly upright and 'Marjorie's Seedling' is even more upright than the gages. A 'Victoria' may be better grown on a longer leg of say 6 ft (1.8 m) to allow for the droop and 'Marjorie's Seedling' could start at 18 in. (45 cm).

Plums have been shown to respond well to tying down of branches, which encourages young vigorous trees to fruit. This is useful when growing the more upright varieties like 'Marjorie's Seedling'. However, heavy cropping reduces the size of the fruit unless it is thinned and may even stop trees growing altogether.

In recent years, the very dwarfing rootstock, Pixy, has become available and should be ideal for growing plums in gardens. Trees can be planted 6½–8 ft (2–2.5 m) apart and trained as open-centre bush or centre-leader trees. They can also be grown as restricted forms. On very fertile soils, Pixy may produce a tree as big as a 'Cox's Orange Pippin' apple on M9, but on poorer soils it makes a weak-growing tree which will require good treatment with mulching and feeding. Most of the vigour problems with trees on Pixy arise because they crop very heavily when still quite young. This can be counteracted by thinning the fruits to singles. It is also important to prune the trees lightly.

DWARF PYRAMID (see figure 16, below, and p. 21)

Plums can be grown as dwarf pyramids by using summer pruning, which not only restricts the size of the tree but also gives the branches greater strength. Trees on both St Julien A and Pixy rootstocks are suitable, but Pixy will require less severe pruning.

Figure 16: dwarf pyramid plum – (*opposite*) first spring after planting; (*below*) subsequent years

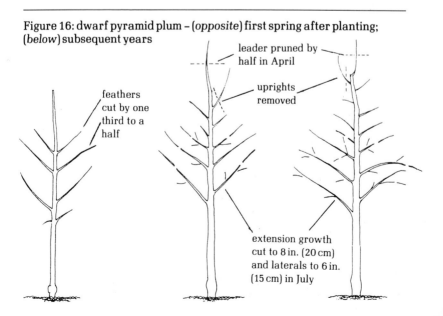

feathers cut by one third to a half

leader pruned by half in April

uprights removed

extension growth cut to 8 in. (20 cm) and laterals to 6 in. (15 cm) in July

After planting in winter, maiden trees are cut to a bud 5 ft (1.5 m) above ground level at flowering time and any feathers cut by a third to half their length. During July, extension growth on the branches is cut back to 8 in. (20 cm) and laterals growing from the branches to 6 in. (15 cm). The extension on the central leader is pruned by half in April the following year.

The shortening of branch extensions and laterals continues in April and July each year, as described above, until the tree has reached the desired height, when the central leader is cut back to the base to contain growth. In the maintenance of dwarf pyramid plums, it is important to ensure that the branches have good light and some removal of branches will be necessary, as well as the removal of any strong upright shoots in summer.

FAN (see figure 17, below, and p. 13)

Trees on St Julien A and Pixy rootstocks can be used to produce a fan-trained tree. The more vigorous St Julien A is best for covering a large space on a wall or trellis.

After planting, an unfeathered maiden tree is headed at flowering time to a bud about 18 in. (45 cm) above the point at which it was grafted. In the spring, buds will begin to break, starting at the top. As the buds break, they are rubbed out until a pair of well placed buds about 1 ft (30 cm) above the union are reached. The subsequent shoots are encouraged to grow by mulching and watering. Once the two shoots have reached 18 in. (45 cm) in length in the summer, they should be tied to two canes fixed to the main support at 45° above the horizontal. The central stem above them is removed and the wound treated with a protective paint.

Figure 17: fan-trained plum – (*below*) first spring and summer after planting; (*opposite*) second and third summer after planting

branches trained
to canes

main stem
removed

upper breaks
removed

selected
shoots
encouraged
to grow

cuts to be made
—45° next March

18 in.
(45 cm)

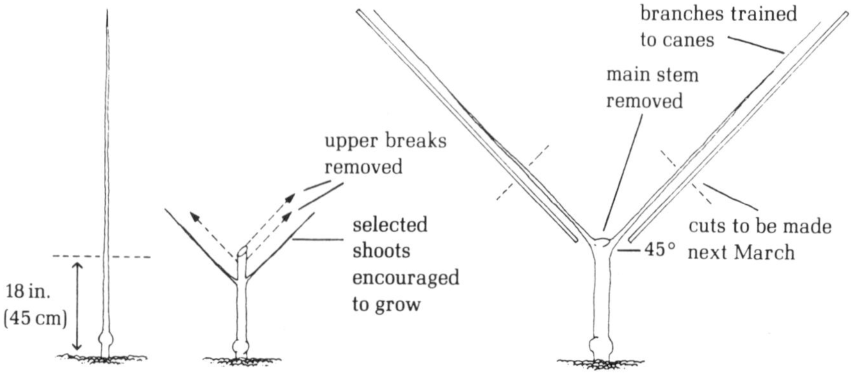

In the case of a feathered maiden, the tree may have two feathers at the place where branches are required and these can be lined up as the tree is being planted and secured to two canes as outlined above. In the April after planting, all other feathers are stubbed back hard. When the pair of branches has grown beyond 18 in. (45 cm), the top of the tree is removed and the wound painted.

The following winter in late February or March, the two retained branches are cut back to 1 ft (30 cm) from the main stem, which should produce four breaks on each one. The building up of the fan proceeds by tying in the leading shoots on the two arms to the 45° canes as they grow; one shoot on the lower side of each arm is secured to a cane at 25° above the horizontal and the other two shoots on each are fixed in more upright positions. Surplus laterals are removed or shortened to five leaves in July.

In the following February or March, these eight leading shoots are cut back to 30 in. (75 cm). The shoots produced as a result of these winter cuts are either tied in to fill space as part of the fan or cut in July to six leaves. After harvest each year, some tidying up will be needed, shortening the summer pruned laterals and removing spent timber and replacing it with younger wood.

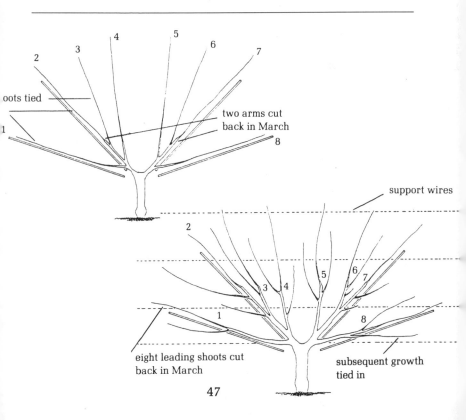

Sweet and Duke Cherries

The rootstocks available for sweet cherries and duke cherries (a cross beween sweet and acid cherries) are F12/1, Colt and Inmil (GM9). Trees on F12/1 become very large and are not suited to the average garden, Colt will produce a tree as big as an apple tree on the rootstock MM106, whereas the new Inmil is said to be dwarfing.

Cherries can be grown in the same forms as plums. The same rules of spring pruning and summer cutting of laterals apply and, with bush and standard forms, little pruning is required after the formative stage. In addition, it is most important to try to avoid narrow angles between branches and the central leader. Not only are narrow angles a source of structural weakness, but they are a danger point for the entry of bacterial canker. Some of the very latest cherries are highly resistant to bacterial canker, but many favourite varieties, including 'Stella', are not.

Sweet cherry 'Merton Bounty' as a fan

Acid Cherries

Although acid or morello cherries can be grown on the same rootstocks as sweet cherries, they always make smaller trees and are therefore more convenient for gardens. However, the fruiting habit is different, the fruit being carried mainly on shoots made the previous year, and presents problems more akin to the peach.

OPEN-CENTRE BUSH AND HALF-STANDARD

After planting, the maiden tree is pruned in late February or March to a bud 43 in. (1.1 m) above ground level, which stimulates growth from around 3 ft (1 m). The feathers or shoots which are required to form the main branches are cut by half each spring for the next two or three years. Once the tree is established and cropping, an annual thinning out of fruited wood and crowded timber is necessary to keep a succession of young growth coming for replacement.

FAN

The formation of a fan is the same as for the peach (see p. 50). In the summer, new growths are selected and tied in and the surplus removed by pinching out. Periodically, some larger pieces of wood should be removed in the spring to revitalize the inner parts of the tree.

A morello cherry on Colt as an open-centre bush

—— Peaches and Nectarines ——

Peaches and nectarines are generally budded on to St Julien A plum rootstock these days, although the more vigorous Brompton is sometimes used. The fan-trained tree is the most popular form for peaches in this country, as it enables trees to benefit from the shelter of a wall. Open-centre bush trees have been grown with mixed success and, on occasion, palmette forms have been used.

FAN

The basic framework of the fan is produced in the same way as for a fan-trained plum. Two side branches from the central stem are cut in February to produce four framework branches on each side and all surplus shoots are pinched out during the summer. In the following late February or March, the eight shoots are headed to 2 ft (60 cm) from their point of origin, making sure that the cut is to a node with a vegetative bud present. Peaches produce both fruit and vegetative buds at the nodes of young shoots, sometimes separately, sometimes in combination. The fruit buds are round, the vegetative buds pointed (see figure 2, p. 9).

During the summer, the young growth produced by the cuts is tied in radially to fill the intervening space, leaving about 4–6 in. (10–15 cm) between shoots. All unwanted or badly positioned shoots must be removed, including breastwood growing out from or into the wall. This is done by pinching out with finger and thumb, starting early in the year when growth is soft and continuing throughout the summer. Any shoots which reach the limit of the allotted space should also have their growing points pinched out. The shoots which have now been tied in are the following year's fruiting wood and, as soon as they reach 18 in. (45 cm), they too have their growing points removed.

Bearing in mind that peaches and nectarines fruit on one-year old wood, the aim each year once the tree is established is to provide a succession of replacement wood. While the fruiting lateral is flowering and cropping, new shoots are allowed to grow from its base, tip and middle. The shoot growing from half-way up is kept as a reserve and then removed once the base shoot is well established and all other shoots, except the extension growth at the end, are pinched out early while still soft, leaving no more than one

A peach fan in bloom

or two leaves. The fruits on a peach tree must also be thinned to a
final spacing of 10 in. (25 cm) apart. This operation is often
performed in stages, starting at the beginning of June and finishing
at the end of the month. The replacement shoot at the base of the
fruiting wood is tied in parallel to it and the replacement extension
shoot may also be tied in if there is enough room, or otherwise cut to
five or six leaves (see figure 18, below).

After harvesting, the fruited wood is cut back to the base shoots,
which are tied in to become the next year's fruiting wood. Unless a
shoot in a tree has a future role for space-filling, extension or
fruiting, it must be removed at the same time.

Figure 18: peach pruning

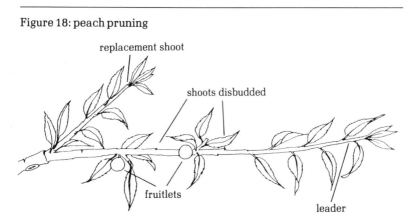

Raspberries

The most popular raspberries are summer-fruiting and crop in high summer on laterals from canes produced the previous year. They need shelter from wind and firm support to prevent damage to the canes, laterals and fruit.

Raspberry canes can be planted between November and March when weather permits. Varieties like 'Glen Clova', which are prolific in canes, should be spaced at 2 ft (60 cm) intervals. Others such as 'Jewel' produce only moderate amounts of cane and are planted 18 in. (45 cm) apart to ensure sufficient canes to tie in for cropping. After planting, cut all canes back to 10 in. (25 cm). During the summer after planting, the 10 in. (25 cm) lengths of cane will produce some laterals, which may even flower and fruit, although it is better not to let them do so. The canes are left untouched until suckers emerge from below ground to become new canes, when the old ones are cut off at ground level (see figure 19, p. 54).

METHODS OF SUPPORT AND TRAINING (see figure 20, p. 54)

It is essential that raspberry canes are well supported with a post-and-wire system. The wires should be 12 gauge galvanized fencing quality or similar and the support posts must be strong and firmly anchored, with not more than 20 ft (6 m) between posts down the row. If the end posts are substantial and the wires can be properly tightened, intermediate posts should not be needed.

The support posts should be 8 ft (2.5 m) long with 2 ft (60 cm) in the ground and wires fixed at 2 ft (60 cm), 3½ ft (1.1 m) and 5¼ ft (1.6 m). There are no hard and fast rules and the height of the wires can be adjusted according to the length of the canes and height of the picker. It should be possible to tighten the wires from one end.

Canes are secured to the wires as soon as they are long enough in the first year or, in later years, immediately after harvest and removal of the old fruited canes. Sometimes fruits can be damaged by the young canes being blown about in strong winds: a length of string tied to the posts and run outside the loose canes can be made tight enough to prevent the worst damage.

Well trained raspberry canes

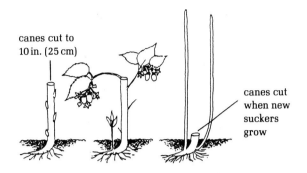

Figure 19: raspberries – (*left*) at planting; (*centre and right*) first summer

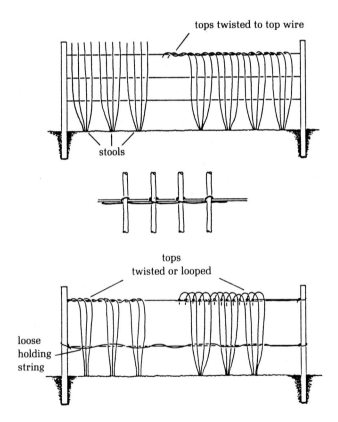

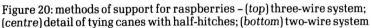

Figure 20: methods of support for raspberries – (*top*) three-wire system; (*centre*) detail of tying canes with half-hitches; (*bottom*) two-wire system

When removing old fruited canes, cut them cleanly to ground level to reduce the risk of disease. The new canes can be tied in individually, using soft fillis, polypropylene baler twine or similar and spacing them 4–6 in. (10–15 cm) apart. Alternatively, each cane can be fixed in position with a length of string, making a series of half-hitches to loop cane and wire together. This is quicker than making individual ties but requires a little practice. The canes are then cut back to 4 in. (10 cm) above the top wire. A modification to this, particularly with a tall variety like 'Leo', is to twist the tops of the canes round the top wire to form a rope. This is done in late summer, when the canes bend and twist quite easily. The presence of a few leaves does not matter.

Another method of support uses only two wires, fixed at 2 ft (60 cm) and 5 ft (1.5 m). The canes are held to the bottom wire with a length of polypropylene string at the same level, tying it to the wire at intervals. The tops of the canes are either twisted round the top wire or looped and tied to it.

Once raspberries are planted, the root system spreads and suckers appear some distance from the original cane. Canes beneath or close to the support system can be used, but those growing far away cannot and have to be removed. In all methods, canes are best confined to the stool, for unwanted canes allowed to grow full length compete with the plant. If all suckers arising away from the stool are cut off as they appear, the plant becomes stronger and produces not only plenty of canes but better crops.

AUTUMN-FRUITING RASPBERRIES

Autumn-fruiting raspberries fruit on the tops of the current season's growth. Most start to crop in September and continue until bad weather spoils the fruit, although 'Autumn Bliss' begins fruiting in mid-August and may finish in time.

Canes of autumn-fruiting raspberries are planted at 18 in. (45 cm) spacing and treated as for summer-fruiting varieties. The young canes of the first summer will flower and fruit in the first autumn. They will need some support, which can be provided by using end posts and polypropylene string to surround the canes. No tying in is necessary. Unlike summer-fruiting raspberries, the old canes must not be cut down immediately after harvesting, but should be left until they are completely dormant and cut to the ground in the winter. Early cutting would produce undesirable regrowth.

– Blackberries and Hybrid Berries –

Blackberries and hybrid berries can be grown on roughly the same principles. Hybrid berries, of which the best known example is 'Loganberry', are derived from crosses involving blackberries or dewberries and raspberries. Like blackberries, most produce long rods of growth, which require support when cropping, although a few grow more like raspberries.

Blackberries and hybrid berries obtained as one-year old plants are planted between autumn and March, cut down to 10 in. (25 cm) and then treated as for raspberries (see p. 53). Pot-raised plants can be planted as soon as the site is prepared. In this case, the plants are not pruned at planting and all leaves are retained.

Blackberries and hybrid berries vary enormously in vigour, with the blackberry 'Bedford Giant' requiring 15 ft (4.5 m) and 'Tayberry' 8 ft (2.5 m) space in the row. For many gardens, very vigorous blackberries may be a difficult proposition.

METHODS OF SUPPORT AND TRAINING (see figure 21, p. 58)

Blackberries and hybrid berries can be trained on walls or over other supports or along a post-and-wire system of the type used for raspberries. Whichever method is used, space must be allowed so that the new young growth can be trained away from or above the older fruiting canes, to reduce the risk of disease spreading and make handling easier.

Fan
Fan-training can be used for varieties of limited vigour or with a habit more like that of the raspberry, such as 'Tayberry' and 'Loganberry'. As for raspberries, a rigid post-and-wire structure is essential. The fan is fixed to the two lower wires and the new canes are tied up and along the top wire.

Rope
The same wire arrangement used in fan-training can be used for the rope method, which is suitable for varieties with flexible canes.

'Loganberry' trained over an archway

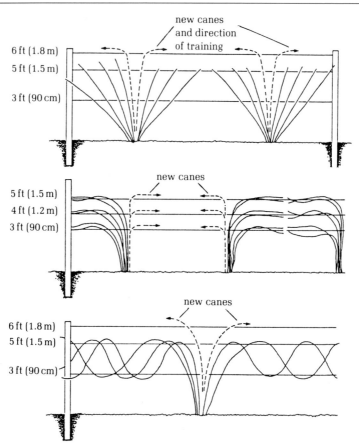

Figure 21: training of blackberries – (*top*) fan-trained; (*centre*) alternate bay method; (*bottom*) weaving method

Fruiting canes are tied in clusters to the two lower canes and again the young canes are trained up the centre and along the top wire.

The alternate bay method is a variation on rope-training. Three wires carry the fruiting canes in one direction only and allow the young canes to be trained in during the growing season in the vacant bay.

Weaving
Very vigorous blackberries can be trained with the weaving technique, although the thorns on some varieties mean that this method is only for the brave. The weaving enables very long canes to be concertinaed into a shorter run. Two wires carry the woven canes for fruiting and a third wire carries the new growth.

Black Currants

Black currants fruit on young wood made the previous year, so it is essential to maintain good growth by pruning and feeding. The varieties vary greatly in vigour and size, from the vigorous 'Wellington' and 'Jet' to the small bush of 'Ben Sarek'. 'Wellington' needs 5 ft (1.5 m) and 'Ben Sarek' 3 ft (1. m) space in the row.

Bushes should be planted so that the bases of the young shoots are below soil level. Traditionally, two-year old bushes are used, but well grown one-year old bushes are perfectly satisfactory. In addition, black currants can easily be raised from cuttings inserted direct into the permanent fruiting position. At planting, all shoots are usually cut down to one bud above ground level, but there is no long-term advantage in doing so. Unpruned bushes establish just as well and can be thinned hard the following winter.

Winter pruning of an established bush consists of cutting out a proportion of the older wood, which is distinguished by its darker colour from the young wood. The amount of wood removed need not exceed a quarter of the total, but much will depend on how the bush has cropped and aged. Bearing in mind that the fruit is produced on young wood, constant rejuvenation is needed. However, in years when spring frosts affect cropping, the short pieces of young wood on three- and four-year old branches will carry crop, although the strong young one- and two-year old shoots have none. There is no advantage in very hard pruning and overstimulating the bush, when light pruning and a little fertilizer will give better results.

The main cuts should be made at ground level, but some thinning of the outer parts of main branches is useful in letting light into the bush. If a bush is very dense, shoots growing from the base often fail to develop and become infected with disease and die back. When bushes are cropping heavily, some branches are pulled to the ground. Since low branches have little future, they can be cut off at harvest time to make picking easier and reduce winter pruning. The rest of the bush will benefit from the reduction in competition.

Certain varieties are particularly inclined to flop under the weight of crop and 'Wellington' tends to spread so much that, if all the low branches were removed to the base, the bush would be decimated. In such a case, the low branches can be cut to a more upright lateral (dehorned). The heavy-cropping 'Ben Sarek' should be mulched, fertilized and watered, but not pruned hard.

Red and White Currants

White and pink currants are sports of the red currant and, as such, are treated in the same way. Unlike black currants, all fruit mainly on short spurs. They can be grown in bush or cordon forms and can be trained as fans, espaliers or palmettes in the same way as tree fruits. Propagation is comparatively easy from hardwood cuttings with all the buds removed except the top three or four. The removal of the lower buds is to prevent suckering and to create a short leg of clean stem, while the top buds will produce the four main branches.

OPEN-CENTRE BUSH

Red and white currant bushes can be bought as one- or two-year olds. The advantage of buying the larger two-year old bush is that it saves time in the formation of the bush and reaching full cropping.

After planting a two-year old bush in winter, all shoots suitable for branch formation are shortened by one third, cutting to an outward-facing bud. A one-year old bush with fewer shoots will need harder cutting to produce the breaks needed and each shoot will have to be reduced by half. About eight branches are required for the traditional open-centre bush.

Each winter as the bush develops, the leading shoots on the main branches are cut by one third and all laterals are cut back to ¾ in. (2 cm) to encourage the development of spurs. Occasionally, an old unfruitful branch may have to be replaced by a young lateral shoot. If the bush becomes too crowded, it should be summer pruned by shortening the laterals to three or five leaves. The time for summer pruning is not critical, but it is best done when the wood has ripened and the crop is nearly ready for harvest. The removal of dense leaves will also make picking easier. In the winter, the summer pruned laterals are then spurred back as before.

STOOLED BUSH

Although red currants are usually grown as open-centre bushes which are close-spur pruned, it is also practical to grow them as stooled bushes in the same way as black currants (see p. 59). The pruning is lighter than for the open-centre bush and is confined to the occasional removal of a branch and spacing out.

CORDON

Red and white currants can be grown as a cordon in single, double or treble form with about 13 in. (35 cm) between the rods. A post-and-wire structure is needed to support the canes used in training the cordon and for its later support. The top support wire should be at about 5 ft (1.5 m), with a further wire at 6½ ft (2 m) to carry a bird protection net if required. Cordon currants are usually trained vertically, but can be grown as oblique cordons.

After planting, the shoot (or shoots, in the case of a multiple cordon) selected to form the central leader is cut by one third and all other shoots removed. The leader is tied to the support cane as soon as practical and encouraged to grow in the direction required but left unpruned. When it reaches 5 ft (1.5 m), it is stopped by summer pruning to five leaves and further shortened in the winter by pruning to one bud.

Laterals are summer pruned each year to five leaves to encourage the development of spurs and are periodically cut back hard in the winter to shorten and rejuvenate the structures. The level of cutting depends on the spacing of the rods.

Cordon red currants (right) and gooseberries (left)

Gooseberries

Gooseberries can be propagated and grown in the same way as red currants. Like them, they can be close-spur pruned and are therefore comparatively easy to train as cordons, espaliers and fans. The big problem with gooseberries lies in their thorns.

OPEN-CENTRE BUSH

There is some variation in the habit of gooseberries. Varieties such as 'Leveller' have a drooping weak habit, while 'Whinham's Industry' is more upright. The new 'Invicta' is vigorous and upright in many situations, but in the early years in exposed sites can become quite prostrate. Firm pruning will keep a bush upright, whereas light pruning and heavy cropping will lead to a more drooping habit.

Traditionally, gooseberries are grown on a short leg of 4–6 in. (10–15 cm). They can be purchased as one-, two- or three-year old bushes, with the one-year old having an average of three shoots and the older bushes up to ten. There are obvious advantages in planting an older bush with the beginnings of a framework.

A one-year old bush should have the young shoots cut by half at planting in autumn or winter. On older bushes, choose six shoots as future branches and cut by one third to a bud pointing in the right direction: drooping shoots should be cut to an upward-facing bud, fairly upright shoots to an outward-facing bud, to counteract any tendency of the branches to flop. All other shoots apart from the six are removed. During the summer, the leaders are encouraged to grow in the desired direction and can even be helped by the use of canes. Any surplus laterals are cut to five leaves.

In the winter, the leaders are again cut by one third and all laterals reduced to one bud. It is important to keep the centre of the bush open, to make picking easier. To maintain the 'bush on leg' form, any shoots from the leg and below ground level must always be removed at the first opportunity.

Above: a fan-trained gooseberry
Below: cordon apples

To keep an established bush in good shape, some summer pruning will be needed in most years. The best time is close to picking or at the actual time of picking, when a pair of secateurs is a useful aid to find a way into a crowded bush. Laterals are usually cut to five leaves, but some can usefully be reduced to a single leaf.

Gooseberries can be grown as open-centre bushes on longer legs up to 4 ft (1.25 m). They may be trained up from a one-year old bush, using a cane to keep the leg straight and forming the head at the height required. Laterals produced on the leg will have to be pinched out as they start.

STOOLED BUSH

It is possible to grow gooseberries as stooled bushes in the same way as the black currant (see p. 59). Picking can be difficult unless the branches are well spread. Most stooled gooseberries happen by accident or neglect, but there is some justification for the practice if there is a persistent problem of botrytis infection of the wood: it is possible to lose a complete bush when the leg becomes infected, but on a stooled bush only a part dies.

CORDON

Gooseberries can be grown as a cordon against a fence or wall or secured to a post-and-wire structure. A cane is necessary to guide the leading shoot in the right direction. The spacing of cordons is 13 in. (35 cm) between rods and they may be vertical or oblique.

After planting, a single shoot is selected to form the leader of a single cordon. A multiple cordon will need more careful selection of shoots to give a balanced start. The chosen leader is cut by one third and all other shoots are cut to one bud.

The leader is tied to the cane as it grows and may require a light winter pruning to stimulate more laterals. The cut is simply a light tipping of less than one sixth of the shoot. If a multiple cordon is being grown, a winter pruning may be needed to keep the growth and vigour of each rod in balance. Laterals are summer pruned to five leaves and winter pruned to one or two buds. There can be some expansion of spur systems outwards, but the picking problem must be considered before allowing too much congestion.

Once the cordon has reached its limit, the leader is summer pruned as a lateral. Any overvigorous shoots which grow on the cordon at any point are best removed completely. (See also p. 61).